# The changing face of
# Manchester
## VOLUME 2

*A special publication brought to you by*

In memory of Lizzi and George

© Manchester Evening News
First published in 2006 by:
MEN Syndication, 164 Deansgate, Manchester, M3 3RN
In conjunction with At Heart Publications
32 Stamford Street, Altrincham, Cheshire, WA14 1EY

ISBN 1-84547-104-0

Printed in Poland by Polskabook

# The city of Manchester has a forever-changing skyline

Having started as a booming home for the age of cotton, it has become one of the country's top city centres boasting Manhattan style skyscrapers and a number of top cultural buildings.

Deansgate at its junction with Whitworth Street West in 1910 and how it looks today.

The 1996 IRA bomb meant much of the city centre was destroyed beyond repair and after a number of years of construction work, Manchester can now again be proud of the many new buildings that have emerged and the historic sites that have been retained.

A quick glance around uncovers the Urbis centre, Radisson Edwardian Hotel, Harvey Nichols, Beetham Tower and the new-look Arndale Centre.

With this in mind the Manchester Evening News has again gone back in time to look at how the city and its surrounding areas looked in the late 19th and 20th century, and how it is today.

Using an immense archive of unique images at the Manchester Evening News combined with a vast quantity of photographs from the city's Central Library we have revisited some of the main places of Manchester to see how they have developed.

Some are almost identical to how they appeared 50 or 60 years ago but some have changed beyond recognition, with thriving modern city life having replaced the old horse and carts of yesteryear.

This second volume of 'The Changing Face of Manchester' takes you back to the good old days of Manchester through these exclusive photographic images accompanied by fascinating tales of how the city has transformed, with a breakdown of what remains and what is new.

It is the best way to see how Manchester has always strived to be a major British city centre, whether it be through the historic golden days of the cotton industry and steam trains or as the top cultural and business hub that it has now become.

Delve inside to see how Manchester was then - and is now!

**Wayne Ankers**
Syndication Editor
Manchester Evening News

# Bombings links two separate eras

Back in 1895, Market Place in the heart of Manchester presented a very picturesque scene - well before the wholesale modernisation of the city centre.

Today, the same area has the delights of retail giants Marks & Spencer and high street fashion outlet Harvey Nichols hoping to lure thousands more shoppers and visitors to the city every day. But, while the secrets of a rich architectural inheritance are mostly hidden, these images neatly bring together both the evidence of the landmarks that have disappeared with those that have survived. The older picture shows a time when Market Place was surrounded by gabled, half-timbered shops and inns, with the tower of the Royal Exchange a prominent landmark in the distance. It is, however, ironic that the up-to-date picture retains an unwelcome link with the past that has visited the area more than once - bombing. In roughly the same location, some Victorian buildings were lost in the bombing raids of 1940 during the Second World War,

after they in turn had replaced medieval constructions. But more dramatic changes came on June 15 1996, when a terrorist bomb exploded in the city centre at the south end of nearby Corporation Street, causing severe damage to many surrounding buildings. The rebuilding after the IRA bombing outrage unleashed a tidal wave of development, which in turn sent similar ripples all across the city that are still continuing today.

# late 1800s

## Class act of the retail royalty

Even in the late 19th Century, Manchester's prestige King Street shopping district was all the rage - and not a lot has changed.

The city centre location has always pulsated to a commercial beat and has, for more than a century, kept a special lustre rivalling addresses like London's Mayfair and New York's Fifth Avenue. Here, the older image of King Street, in 1892, has a graceful, almost Dickensian charm, with buildings to reflect the bourgeoning affluence of the times.

The impressive three and four-storey buildings on both sides of the road are still in place, to help maintain King Street's showpiece façade. In the distance, looking beyond Cross Street, lies a crowded banking and financial quarter, with its own interesting history.

# New face of street where tragedy struck

The photographs may be separated by more than 100 years but some things haven't changed in this image of Manchester city centre.

Oldham Street today and in 1894 is full of hustle and bustle as people go about their business. But the building on the right, which has now been converted into an amusement arcade, has a tragic past. It was home to the former Woolworth's store, which caught fire more than 25 years ago claiming the lives of 10 people. They perished within minutes after inhaling the poisonous fumes given off from

the furniture department during the blaze in May 1979. Horrifying images of staff trapped behind security bars gasping for air as they waited for firefighters to free them were shown around the world. The tragedy led to new safety laws, banning the use of certain dangerous materials in the manufacture of furniture. Now the former Woolworth's store is part of the Northern Quarter, which has seen a multi-million pound transformation in recent years. The district has become a magnet for a diverse range of companies - from design studios and specialist music shops to independent bars and restaurants.

# Survivor of the Blitz, but not march of time

The dramatic transformation of Manchester city centre is graphically illustrated in these two photos.

Horse-drawn trams wind their way in front of the imposing Victoria Buildings - an office, shopping and hotel complex opened in Deansgate in the 1880s.

One tram is carrying an advert for soap from the famous Port Sunlight factory on the Wirral. The people in this picture, taken in 1895, would not recognise modern Manchester with its designer

shops and expensive flats. But some older readers may remember firefighters battling a blaze at the building when it was severely damaged by German bombs in the Blitz. Today's image is dominated by the swanky apartment block, No1 Deansgate, where a penthouse home sells for more than £1m.

# Pubs and publishers

The junction of Great Ancoats Street and Oldham Road, in Ancoats, is famous as being the site of the distinctive all-glass Express Newspapers building.

The building once housed hundreds of journalists and printers who worked on the Daily and Sunday Express and, following its launch in 1979, the Daily Star. Until recently, newspaper staff would pour out day and night to refresh themselves at the Crown & Kettle pub, which stood next door-but-one, on the corner. How different was the scene in 1895; the horse-drawn tram

destination Newton Heath, a couple of miles up Oldham Road, proudly advertises Bryant & May matches and Ogden's cigarettes opposite Luna Street. There's no sign of a newspaper publishers or a pub, for that matter.

# The 'scent of renewal'

Back in 1849 a commentator identified the new district of Hulme as the most salubrious of Manchester's working class areas with "humble but comfortable streets".

In many ways, the story of this fascinating inner city area is one of rolling change. And as these images show, the transformation continues apace to this day. The junction of Chorlton Road and Stretford Road has not altered much in shape - a main corridor into Manchester city centre with housing on both sides of a busy thoroughfare. In one picture terraced housing,

transport and business all vie for room in the wide space, while the same spot today stands as a hallmark to the trend-setting makeover Hulme has had over the last few years. Going back in time, names like the Golden Eagle Hotel and the Stretford Road Hotel will doubtless bring back memories for some and local history enthusiasts will be interested to know that back in 1896 Stretford Road was renowned for Marks and Sparks and the first penny bazaar. Today, after a struggle, the once run-down area has finally rid itself of the notorious 1970s deck-access flats which to many became sad symbols for the mistakes of post-war social housing. Now stimulated by the scent of renewal, new two and three-bedroom homes are only a small part of the regeneration programme that has changed the look of the area beyond recognition.

# Days of two horsepower transport

Open-topped trams pulled by horses were a familiar sight in Victorian Manchester.

But in 1898 this cheap form of transport also brought with it an easy pace at which to take in the beautiful Victorian architecture that could be seen all around the north Manchester district of Blackley. Typically, everyone caught on camera in the old picture, including the little boy at the front of the tram, is wearing a hat - from the working man's flat cap and

the gent's bowler, to the boater-style head gear worn by the conductor. Dominating the up-to-date picture is the The Farmyard pub, on Rochdale Road. It is a good example of the sturdy durability of some of the buildings in the area. Despite many internal and external alterations over the years, the building has retained its eye-catching architecture and striking frontage and still overlooks a busy bus route, although the tram tracks have long gone. In stark contrast, the building jutting out further down on the left of the picture is a modern leisure centre, a striking, angled building but, arguably, possessing none of the grand style of The Farmyard. The terrace of homes on the right has been replaced by a swathe of grass and houses set back from the road.

# Cooks and books

Generations of Manchester's residents and students have used Central Library, which has become one of the city's most famous and best-loved landmarks.

But many are surprised to discover the library was built as recently as 1934. Features of its neo-classical style lead people to believe Central Library is a much older building than it actually is. The image on the left shows Peter Street looking towards Deansgate in 1904. The Midland Hotel is on the left and what is now the site of the Central Library used to be the location of the Waldorf Restaurant. These two establishments would have been a focal point for social events in the heart of Manchester, but while the Midland would continue to wine and dine residents and visitors for many years to come, the Waldorf Restaurant would become a magnet for books, not cooks. In 1911 Manchester Free Library occupied temporary premises in Piccadilly Gardens. Powers for a compulsory purchase of a site were provided in the Manchester Corporation Act of 1920. A suitable plot was identified in St Peter's Square, which would also be used for an

extension to Alfred Waterhouse's magnificent town hall. A competition was held and Vincent Harris's designs for both buildings were accepted. Prime Minister Ramsay McDonald laid the foundation stone for the library in 1930 and it was finally opened by King George V in 1934, the town hall extension opening four years later.

# 1900-19

## The more things change...

More than 100 years might have passed, but - incredibly, particularly in this day and age - the buildings have remained almost unchanged in appearance.

In 1900, this corner of Cateaton Street and Victoria Street was a bustling thoroughfare, populated by families out for a stroll, shoppers and a scurrying horse and cart. In 2005, sadly, the colourful shops have almost all gone, or at least are permanently boarded up.

# A saintly place

Over 100 years ago, this busy part of Oxford Road, Manchester, was known as All Saints - as it is today.

Then, of course, the cobbled road was full of horse-drawn wagons and trams, one of which was making its way to Withington, judging by the picture.

The area to the left of the picture was Grosvenor Square, with the classical portico of Chorlton-on-Medlock town hall in Cavendish Street - now part of Manchester Metropolitan University, as is

the building alongside it, the
Manchester College of Art,
where L S Lowry was a student.

# The lost city

Back in 1900, going to Manchester's Shudehill area was reckoned to be a thrilling "trip to town" - because it provided a welcome break for visitors hungry for the excitement of the city centre.

Today, a passing glance at this historic section of the Northern Quarter wouldn't be complete if it didn't include the marketplaces of Smithfields/Shudehill, a robust trade district and an early centre for popular literature - a tradition continued today by Frontline Books on nearby Newton Street. Picture the scene in 1900: the public houses are

roaring full, the streets are swarming with men and women, and the shouts and laughter of girls and boys mingle with the music that floats out of pub windows. Strange how this city centre culture has hardly changed in more than a century, and the current focus on the night-time economy is as vital today as it was in Victorian times. The cobbled streets have gone and only a few buildings around Shudehill have retained their stuccoed warehouse look - in stark contrast to the towering CIS building punctuating the skyline. Where imposing architecture boasting graceful cast-iron columns once stood, the CIS looms large, overlooking the changes to an area that remains a mecca for business, trade - and enjoyment.

# 1900-19

# Cool spot that's hot

With Manchester ranked as a leading retail destination, glitzy Exchange Square, in the heart of the city, has always had stylish aspirations.

In fact, the bright new development, renowned for attracting top stores like Selfridges, is typical of the pulling power and multi-million-pound investment that endows the area with an enduring feeling of prosperity. The 21st century gimmickry, designed to make the area throb to the beat of a modern city, may not be to the taste of all visitors, but the new

space has been applauded by thousands of people hunting the coolest products from top names. Although most of the cosy Edwardian interior of the Corn Exchange has been lost, shoppers now have a rich array of choice.

# 1900-19

## A Swan song...

In 1900 the bustling Swan Street area of Manchester had all the hallmarks of a typical Victorian market - with men in flat caps and ladies in long dresses filling the cobbled streets.

Fittingly, the city's then rapid development and bourgeoning reputation for commerce was soon to see the first electric tram run just a year later. Swan Street was renowned for a fascinating mix of businesses, including a herring and egg merchant, glass works, oyster dealers, tobacconist, jewellers, pawnbrokers, and instrument makers. The archive picture of

Swan Street looking towards Rochdale Road is as full of atmosphere and endeavour as optimism for the growth of the city's increasing financial prowess. While Swan Street is unrecognisable today, with a wide three-lane road and painted white buildings in place of red brick, a glance upwards shows that some of the structures retain the bold architecture of its glorious past.

# Where traffic now rules

It would not be good idea to stop for a chat today at the spot where the men and boys of 1902 are gathered in our picture from the past.

The urinal and fountain in the photograph of New Cross, Ancoats, at the junction of Oldham Road and Great Ancoats Street, have gone and you would be risking serious injury trying to stroll around this area today. It is now one of Manchester's busiest junctions and thousands of cars pass through daily. Ancoats was once the centre of the

world's cotton industry which
attracted a huge influx of
Italian migrants and created
what became known as
Manchester's Little Italy. In
more recent years the area
was also home to hundreds of
journalists as Manchester
gained the reputation as the
Fleet Street of the north.

# Style's still in tune

More than 100 years separate these two images of Crumpsall - but nothing can diminish one of Manchester's finest examples of Victorian style and longevity.

The long, leafy avenues and rambling period houses now converted into apartments are just some of the signs that Crumpsall has survived and thrived as an attractive residential district.

In fact, two of Manchester's most senior politicians, MP Graham Stringer and Manchester city council leader Richard Leese, still live in the area, and in the 19th century,

Polish-French composer Frederic Chopin is reputed to have stayed in a house at the top of Crumpsall Lane.

Crumpsall has had its share of setbacks, but the area boasts one of the largest hospitals (North Manchester General) and in Crumpsall Lane itself, the highly-regarded Crumpsall Lane Primary School, housed in a grand red-brick 19th century Manchester Corporation building.

Close by is Crumpsall Park - now revamped thanks to the efforts of the Friends of Crumpsall Park.

# Mighty mills loom in the gloom

The awesome sight of huge cotton mills with chimneys so tall they outstripped the church spires is not obvious from these bleak and uninspiring images of Ancoats.

But their place on the banks of the Rochdale Canal is at least testament to their architectural longevity, when all around an air of dereliction hovers, and nearby cleared sites hint more at neglect than restoration. The older image, taken in 1903, is of McConnel and Kennedy's Mills, in Redhill Street, then called Union Street, with Murray's Mills close by.

McConnel & Kennedy built their first cotton-spinning factory in Ancoats in 1798 - employing more than 1,500 workers in 1836 - and were responsible for the first successful application of steam power to mule spinning. The mills were also among the earliest to be lit by gas - just one example of the superiority McConnel & Kennedy had over neighbouring mills.

Interestingly, the Murray brothers - Adam and George - who owned the mill nearest to McConnel & Kennedy, not only originated from Kirkcudbrightshire in southern Scotland like their rivals, but were apprenticed to the same textile machine manufacturer.

# 1900-19

# A city pooling its wealth

Cheetham Hill Road baths in 1903, below, were a tell-tale sign that increased manufacturing and wealth were having a positive impact on Manchester's standard of living a century ago.

Swimming became a leisure treat for all the family to enjoy together, as other improved amenities sprouted up all around. Schools, hospitals, libraries, public wash-houses and swimming baths could all be afforded as a municipal duty and paid for out of rates. Although some deplored the public expenditure as "expensive and unnecessary luxuries",

it didn't prevent councillors announcing plans to provide baths to three other wards - Longsight, St Luke's and Rusholme. Over the years, many children learned to swim at the Cheetham Hill baths, often walking there straight from the local schools. But ambitious building projects didn't stop at swimming baths. Manchester not only started to see the installation of clean water and sewers due to the laying of a pipeline to the Lake District, but gas, electricity and electric trams were soon added to the city's amenities. Today, the site of the old baths is occupied by rows of flats.

# 1900-19

# Changes we have to grin and Bear

Outstanding signs of Edwardian architecture have survived for more than 100 years in the heart of Manchester city centre.

A typical example is the still elegant building on the corner of Market Street near Piccadilly, an imposing presence in the bustling business district. Thankfully, restoration by modern day architects and planners have kept faith with the style and look of the multi-storey structure that dates back to 1903 in the older image. Names like RB Grover have

been replaced by a Starbucks Coffee outlet, but the overall shape and appearance of the building have valiantly survived a century of change. Today, the edge of Piccadilly Gardens is awash with banks, offices and commercial buildings, and roads dissected by tram tracks that ferried people across the city in the early part of the last century. Close inspection of the other buildings nearby reveals the historic names of grocers T Seymour Meade, who had shops all over the north west, and the impressive White Bear Hotel. This was a popular inn dating back to the middle of the 19th century. Sadly, the period architecture of the building has been erased and replaced by a bland substitute.

# Squaring up to new challenges

The size and setting of Manchester's St Peter's Square represents everything our city fathers had always strived for – a lasting symbol of industrial achievement and trading prowess.

In fact, few people would argue that the square, standing at the heart of Manchester's civic and public life, illustrates the wealth and importance of the city in the early 20th century as much as it does today. But would those same city fathers have allowed a purposefully-constructed urban space – and the even grander buildings that surround it

– to be so dominated by traffic, thus creating the intrusion of noise and pollution to, arguably, make it look and feel a less appealing enclosure? Fortunately, the buildings we see in both old and new images of St Peter's Square still go some way to sustaining the city's sense of identity and quality. Conservation Area status also helps to safeguard the surrounding imposing structures. In 1907, the year a public square was formed, there was still no Central Library. That didn't open until 1934, and immediately challenged the nearby Midland Hotel for architectural plaudits. The library – a magnificent circular building with a huge portico supported by six Corinthian columns – has earned its reputation as one of the great monuments of Manchester.

# Gorton's dark past

Gorton became noteworthy in 1636, when Samuel Gorton, a clothier born in the district, sailed to America, fearing religious persecution.

There he founded a sect called the Gortonites, whose members were regularly thrashed for religious dissent. The older picture shows Corporation Street, now known as Constable Street, as viewed from Ashton Old Road in 1908. Abbey Hey Lane curves behind it. In the year the picture was taken, Gorton hit the headlines when the Prince Of Wales Hotel, on

Abbey Hey Lane, became the scene of a double murder. John Ramsbottom, son-in-law of the licensee, shot his wife in the chest, before shooting her brother. The dim square at the end of the unpaved street was Gorton New Mill, also on Abbey Hey Lane, opened in 1858 by John Buckley, a brewer. The factory employed 200 workers, two-thirds of them women. Many would have got their lunch from the bakers in Bread Street, just off Constable Street, quenched their thirst at the Prince Of Wales and repented afterwards at St George's Church, Abbey Hey Lane. Twenty years after this picture was taken, the mill, full of bales of cotton, was destroyed in a massive blaze. People came from all over Manchester to watch the fire. The picture, below right, shows Constable Street today. The canal has been filled in and the site of Gorton New Mill is green space. A number of the shops that served the mill workers are still there, though under different ownership. The area is more residential than industrial, but has lost none of its vibrancy. Abbey Hey Lane is now home to Wright Robinson Sports College and Abbey Hey Primary School.

# Where old meets new

Every picture tells a story, or so the saying goes, and never was that saying more true than with these two photographs.

Below is a 1908 picture of Stockport Road, Plymouth Grove, home to Longsight Meeting Room (left), numerous advertising hoardings and shops, while tram tracks dissect the cobbled road that runs between Toll Gate Close and Hayley Street. Nearly a century later, the only thing left standing is the building housing the meeting rooms,

which – despite its age –
seems to have weathered
better than the more
recently-built two-storey
council properties alongside it.

# 1900-19

# New trends replace the old

Our modern taste for a brew on the go shows itself in stark terms here with a coffee shop built across a side road at the top of Market Street, Manchester.

And the photographs also illustrate the new trend for bargain shopping with TK Maxx in the building which once housed the famous Lewis's department store. But wouldn't Wiles' bazaar be fascinating to walk around?

# Blue Bell rings the changes

Legend has it that the infamous highwayman Dick Turpin once stopped at the Blue Bell Inn at Levenshulme – no doubt in search of a refuge from the law as much as a jug of ale.

While the tale about Turpin may have been fuelled more by myth than fact, the Blue Bell Inn is very real, having survived on the same Barlow Road site as its 1910 predecessor. In fact, the older image of this part of Levenshulme – a rural enclave dating back to the 13th century – shows just how much the industrial revolution took hold of what

was, essentially, a farming community. As the population of Levenshulme grew, the building of railways, mills and factories sounded the death knell for the farmers and their traditional way of life. Levenshulme, about six miles south of the centre of Manchester, was a village in its own right, located on the Manchester to Stockport Road, now known as the A6. Today, the Blue Bell's imposing neo-Georgian facade commands a lot more space and attention than it once did, and is due for more refurbishment soon to secure its place for many more years to come.

# A bridge spanning two eras

Deansgate is almost as old as Manchester itself and, for much of its existence, it has been one of the city's main thoroughfares.

During the Roman occupation, it was the route between river crossings for the Medlock and the Irwell. Its name dates back to Anglo-Saxon times, with some historians saying it relates to a church official, others claiming it points to when the Danes invaded Manchester, and some insisting it means "a road that runs by a river". The older

picture shows Deansgate at its junction with Whitworth Street West in 1910. Horse-drawn carriages and Edwardian cyclists cross the cobbles under the railway bridges, one of which still stands. On the right is the Railway Hotel, the nearest hostelry to what was then Knott Mill Station. It was always busy, as this end of Deansgate was home to many thriving businesses, many connected to the motor trade. In the distance, the distinctive brickwork of the Great Northern Warehouse can be made out. It now houses a cinema, restaurants, estate agents, furniture stores and conference space. Today, as can be seen in our present-day picture, the Railway Hotel is gone. The place where it stood now leads to the G-Mex Metrolink stop, and to the right of it out of view are Deansgate Locks' nightspots. The nearby station has been renamed from Knott Mill to Deansgate.

# Delights of those double-deckers

Public transport in Greater Manchester dates back to the 1820s, when an enterprising businessman started a regular horse bus or coach service to the city centre.

The success of the horse-drawn double-deckers – known as omnibuses – covered most of the main roads in Manchester and in many surrounding districts. But it was more than 50 years later that the tram was unveiled – and it revolutionised travel in Manchester. The older image shows the tram terminus at Palatine Road and Lapwing

Lane, West Didsbury, in 1912. Lapwing Lane runs left to right across the foreground of the picture and the photographer is looking up at Palatine Road towards Withington railway station. The large sign is directing people towards the station. The lightly-used routes in southern Manchester from Palatine Road to Cheadle and Northenden, and Hulme to Chorlton-cum-Hardy, were still being operated by horse buses at the turn of the century. Then the general manager of Manchester Corporation Tramways Department recommended they experiment with motor buses on these services, and they were introduced in 1906. A century later the terminus has been replaced by housing. But trams could be returning to south Manchester – if transport bosses give the green light to a Metrolink extension between Didsbury and Stockport.

# Keeping an eye on the past

It's more than 90 years since this picture from the past was taken, but the façade of Manchester's Royal Eye Hospital has changed little.

The medical technology inside has altered beyond recognition since this scene was captured in 1913, yet the front of the imposing building on Oxford Road appears in much of its original form. Not so the street scene around it, though, where cobbles and horse-drawn carriages have given way to one of the busiest routes into the city

centre. While cars and buses dominate along the road today, it was public transport of a different kind that kept people moving past the hospital then, with tram tracks cutting their way through the cobbles. The scene directly outside the hospital has also altered – the wide pavement on which gentlemen and ladies in hats strolled is now home to two telephone boxes and safety railings to guard pedestrians from today's speedier traffic. The Royal Eye Hospital was founded in 1834 and is now the country's second largest provincial postgraduate teaching hospital with a reputation as a prestigious centre of education and research. It opened Manchester's first eye bank in 1988 with the help of boxer Frank Bruno, who was operated on for a corneal defect by one of the hospital's professors. Today, the Royal Infirmary stands behind the Eye Hospital. When the 1913 picture was taken the building was known as the New Infirmary.

# 1900-19

# Transported in time

This area of London Road, in city centre Manchester, has undergone plenty of changes since the photo was taken in 1914.

However, as one of the main thoroughfares out of town, it has always been a busy place. Today, of course, the trams that made their way into Piccadilly have been replaced by Metrolink trams, and the horse and cart that can be seen trotting below wouldn't stand a chance against the buses and cars of modern-day Manchester. It's interesting to see that the

building just behind the
traffic policeman's head is still
standing; today it houses the
Rossetti Hotel. The companion
building to its right has long
gone, replaced by a modern
and architecturally inferior
row of shops that lead to
Piccadilly Station approach.

# City market traded in for museum

There may be nearly 90 years between these two images, but it appears not much has changed in this corner of Manchester.

The former City Hall, now home to the Air and Space Museum, is the last remaining example of the ornamental ironwork that was the trademark of the Bellhouse family of builders. Constructed in 1877, as the Lower Campfield Market, it was built for Manchester Corporation. It was originally open-sided until near the end of the 19th century, when it

was closed. A gallery was added before it became known, as it is most commonly remembered, as City Hall. The large rectangular building has been modified many times over the years. But the biggest transformation came in 1983. With its ornately-detailed, cast iron and partly-glazed roofs, the old market building was renovated for the display of historic aeroplanes. The work was carried out by acting city architect E Clark for the city council before it became a fundamental part of the Manchester Museum of Science and Industry in 1985. The interior space has been preserved for its present use of housing large classic aircraft which have a special relevance to the city. The exhibits are maintained to illustrate the connection of Manchester with aircraft production.

# Pale shadow of the cosmopolitan past

People forget there was a time when Cheetham and Cheetham Hill were separate entities – because now they're regarded as one and the same.

Contemporary Cheetham is, arguably, only a pale shadow of its former self, and on close inspection found to be a little run-down by modern standards. In fact, the older image showing Waterloo Road and Halliwell Lane back in 1915 – at the junction with Cheetham Hill Road – has an elegance sadly missing from an updated version distinguished only by wide

open spaces. Wide and cobbled roads clearly showing tramlines were once bordered by grand housing compared with the lacklustre scene we see today. The area has, however, retained its reputation for many small retail and wholesale businesses, including clothing, jewellery and furnishing traders. By the middle of the last century, Halliwell Lane was renowned as the place to do the weekly shop, with a number of interesting-sounding retailers who helped give a cosmopolitan flavour to the district. They included Lorenzenes, an Italian ice cream parlour, a French patisserie shop called Rouetes, and Titantics the delicatessen. Those who lived in the Cheetham area at the time might also remember the many shops on Waterloo Road, including Timpson's shoes, the Post Office, a chemist, and several bakers' shops.

# Building Manchester's future

It's fascinating to see how buildings we take for granted were built, generations ago.

The picture on the left – taken in 1935 – shows a section of the UMIST building, on the corner of Whitworth Street and Sackville Street, being erected. In the course of 70 years, very little of this road junction has changed.

The overhead cables have gone, of course, as have the rather quaint bollards.

But, all in all, the passage of time has been kind to this part of Manchester city centre.

# Sign of the times

If ever a picture highlighted dramatic changes in an urban landscape, then this is the one.

On the left is a 1922 photograph of Sandywell Street, taken from Ashton Old Road.

In the right-hand picture, Ashton Old Road is still there – with tram lines and the original cobbles underneath the Tarmac – but everything else has vanished. Not only have the houses and shops gone – to be replaced by featureless maisonettes – but

there is no longer any access to Sandywell Street. The black and white photo is a treasure trove of memories; of the newspapers featured on the advertising hoarding on the corner shop on the right, only the Sunday Times still exists. And on the left, note the traditional pawnbroker's sign, with its distinctive three globes. Today, Ashton Old Road is a busy thoroughfare. All those years ago, it was a different story.

# The hidden gem

It is hard to imagine that just a few hundred metres beyond this unremarkable urban sprawl lies a 300-acre park area where deer herds roamed.

Historic Boggart Hole Clough is within walking distance of the junction of Moston Lane and Clough Road, an area once popular with families attracted to the boating lake and children's play area. The park, arguably one of the jewels in the then Manchester Corporation's crown, boasted pristine bowling greens and an impressive boulevard

stretching into the depth of the park. Today, Boggart Hole Clough, home to the Blackley War Memorial, is classed as one of Manchester's principal parks where the facilities include a bowling green, tennis courts, football pitches, archery, orienteering course, boating lake and athletics track, plus access for disabled people. The park once had a team of 20 gardeners who took care of the grounds but by the 1980s the staff levels were cut to one or two men. Our two images show that the shape of Moston Lane has hardly changed since 1924 where the cobbled streets and two-up, two-down houses were typical of the suburban streets to be found all over Manchester. But on the left close to the Co-operative Wholesale Society building, is a sign for Camp Coffee behind the LS Lowry-style figure. Camp Coffee, a liquid cordial which only needed hot water added, was an acquired taste and is rarely seen today.

# School days

The image on the left is of School Lane, Didsbury, pictured from Winifred Street, looking towards the L.M.S. railway bridge and Didsbury village in 1924.

Notice that in the modern photograph on the right, the old line of the kerbstones can still be seen approaching the narrow bridge.

On the right-hand side, next to the trees, is the red-bricked Baptist church, which is still there, as are the houses on the left-hand side.

Two large blocks of flats now stand on either side of the road near the bridge and

the Pitcher And Piano is on
the right-hand side as you
look towards the village.

## 1920s-30s

# Keeping up with tradition

Napoleon called us a nation of shopkeepers and even a cursory glance at Chester Road, Stretford, at the junction with Taylors Road, over a period of almost 80 years, would tend to confirm his opinion.

In 1926, a parade of shops stood behind the tram shelter. The latter is long gone, but the shops still stand, although much has changed in what they sell. The building on the other side of Taylors Road, seen quite faintly, is St Peter's Church, now demolished.

# District's echoes of Chopin

It may not quite be the leafy retreat it once was, but Crumpsall, in north Manchester, is a fascinating mix of history and heritage.

Composer Frederic Chopin once lived in the area, and it still proudly retains its Victorian credentials in the 21st century.

Although Crumpsall Lane in 1926, pictured below, showing a winding tree-lined cobbled road with large houses on either side, has been replaced by modern semi-detached houses, many other buildings have simply changed with the

times. No reference to the area would be complete without mentioning Abraham Moss, a former Lord Mayor, and one of the city's leading Jewish, civic, educational, and cultural figures. He was chairman of the North Manchester Hospital Management Committee, whose remit included the Jewish Hospital.

# Old glories remain

The cobbles might be long gone, but much of the architecture in Manchester's Portland Street remains just as it was in 1929.

This picture from the past shows the stretch next to Piccadilly Gardens and many of the key landmarks are still there, almost 80 years on. The Thistle Hotel, pictured on the right today with flags proudly flying, has altered little – on the outside at least. But while luxury bedrooms, bars and a restaurant are now inside, it was once home to a firm of linen manufacturers,

merchants and warehousemen. Richardson, Tee, Rycroft & Company was based at mills in Barnsley, South Yorks, but is believed to have used its base in Manchester as a depot. Meanwhile, Clayton House, which is the third building from the left of the picture, also looks the same, with its tall chimneys and ornate frontage. Today, cars, vans and buses queue along what has become one of the busiest routes through the city centre, where roadside parking is a thing of the past. Back in 1929, however, motor cars pulled up on the street, apparently without fear of being booked by eager traffic wardens. For those who relied on public transport, there was refuge in the middle of the carriageway in the form of an ornate glass and metal shelter. But it was not only buses that served this part of the street in 1929. Trams – their tracks and overhead lines clearly visible in the older picture – also helped workers, shoppers and visitors get about town.

# Losing sight of the past

This 1930 picture of Kirkmanshulme Lane, Longsight, taken from Stockport Road, shows how times have changed.

The cobbles have given way to Tarmac, and the old-fashioned street lamp has been replaced by modern lights. And the corner shop, which proudly displays its hoardings advertising Bovril, is long gone.

Then, Kirkmanshulme Lane led travellers to the delights of Belle Vue – with its zoo, amusement park and speedway arena.

Today, only the Belle Vue Aces survive; the roller-coaster has long gone, replaced by homes, a multiplex cinema and an industrial development.

# 1920S-30S

# Transports of delight no longer

Buses and Manchester have connections going back to the 19th century – and no amount of modernisation can deny Hyde Road Bus Depot its proud place in the city's glorious transport history.

Fittingly, on the wall at the entrance of the depot in Ardwick is a war memorial – a large brass plaque erected as a permanent remembrance of the men from Hyde Road who gave their lives during the First World War. Later, the names of those who perished in the Second World War were added. In 2005 the depot, which currently provides bus services to more

than 408,000 passengers a week (a staggering 21 million passenger journeys a year), celebrated its 100th birthday. Originally built in 1903 for trams for Manchester Corporation, with the last tram leaving in 1949, the transformation of the building from imposing red brick with stone dressing, to one of unsubtle blandness, is evident. Nostalgia buffs will recall that between 1937 and 1966, trolley buses operated from the depot. Then followed SELNEC, who operated buses from the depot from 1969, GM Buses from 1974, GM Buses South from 1986 and Stagecoach from 1996. The Shuttle buses for the much-applauded 2002 Commonwealth Games also operated from the Hyde Road depot. Today, the depot operates with more than 200 buses and employs more than 400 people.

# An urban oasis

Work designed to usher the heart of Manchester's Piccadilly into the 21st century has arguably been a mix of success and failure as the city strives to build an open space of international quality.

But there have been tangible gains as city bosses determine to improve the urban environment, particularly the overhaul of Piccadilly Gardens. While the showpiece city-centre garden has undergone a transformation, the newer image shown here indicates that the promise to make the area better for shoppers, visitors, pedestrians and

residents is mostly being adhered to. Buses are still seen zipping through at regular intervals, but the addition of the Metrolink trams is helping return Piccadilly Gardens to its former glory and secure its reputation as a vital hub of the city. The image taken in 1932 has several poignant memory jerkers, including bowler-hatted gentlemen.

At the time the area boasted a famous Lyons cafe, an early Persil washing powder sign and lumbering double-decker buses that would dwarf today's sleeker transport. Meanwhile, the £10m new-look Piccadilly Gardens, now reduced in size and the once sunken garden now levelled, has a route called the catwalk, to parade itself to the world.

# Worlds apart

These contrasting images of north Manchester are worlds apart in time and appearance – but the older picture tells its own intriguing story of life during the Great Depression.

The year is 1934, and Rochdale Road, pictured below at its junction with Queens Road, shows some signs of recovery after the 1929 stock market crash. This led to the worst economic downturn in American history, subsequently spreading to other parts of the world. The Depression did much to slow down Manchester's exuberant population growth, but a close

look at fashions worn by the men and women indicate a degree of returning prosperity. The ladies, dressed in suit coats, and the bowler-hatted men at least give the impression of economic well-being. Austere but stylish, the mood instilled by the Depression was suitably reflected in the preference for dark colours, navy blue, brown and black. Today, this area of

Manchester couldn't look more different – or brighter. New homes – nearly 3,000, mostly private – are concentrated in the Queens Road-Rochdale Road area.

# 1920s-30s

## Road to renewal

It's hard to believe that these two pictures are of the same place, but the photograph below really is Rochdale Road, Collyhurst.

Back in 1934, this part of Manchester was a typically thriving inner-city suburb, with buses, cars and horse-drawn carriages meandering down the cobbled main road, which wends its way to a horizon dotted with chimneys and a spire, Albert Memorial Church. Over seventy years later, things are so different. Where once there were bricks and mortar, now grow trees.

Indeed, it is hard to spot anything in the newer photograph below that survives from pre-war years – apart, of course, from the road, which bends in the same direction.

# Kingsway is now a route for masses

The changing face of south Manchester is shown in these contrasting images. It was all quiet on Kingsway at its junction with Wilmslow Road in Didsbury when the first picture was taken in 1935.

Kingsway was one of the major routes out of the city centre, which was built in the 1920s as dual carriageway tram routes. The clock tower on the left hand side of the picture formed part of the bus depot. However during the last 60 years the area has undergone a dramatic transformation. The bus depot no longer exists and has been replaced by a superstore,

although the clock tower remains. A multi-million pound health club, cinema, restaurants, bowling and bingo complex has also been built. It is a landmark development, based on a unique land-for-buildings deal between Manchester City Council and Thornfield Developments Ltd. Thornfield built a £13m school to replace the Parrs Wood High building, which had stood on the prime site, at no cost to the city. Kingsway has also become one of the city's main transport arteries with thousands of cars using the route everyday.

# Hats off to the old hall

Men in bowler hats standing at the corner of Deansgate and St Mary's Street discussing the day's business are an image of times gone by in Manchester.

They signal the changes that Deansgate has undergone in the past 70 years, evolving from a commercial centre to include leisurely pastimes like dining out and shopping. And the huge five-storey Houldsworth Hall, which dominates the earlier picture, also has a long and colourful past. The busy and vibrant corner facade of the historic hall has become a

more anonymous, whitewashed frontage. And though, nowadays, shoppers pass by the building on their way to Kendals, it played a key part in Manchester's social history during the 20th century. During the Second World War it became a temporary home to the Manchester Reform Synagogue for seven years until 1948, when the group moved back to their original building on Park Place. It also accommodated the BBC Philharmonic Symphony Orchestra for a brief period, as well as being a key site for anti-fascist protests in the 1970s. More recently, ex-Rolling Stones guitarist Bill Wyman opened a second branch of his famous Sticky Fingers restaurant at the site in 1996. But, even after visits from stars like David Beckham and Barry Manilow, it closed in 1999. Now the corner frontage of Houldsworth Hall is dominated by the Italian restaurant Bella Pasta, adding to the growing number of dining venues on Deansgate.

# Stops and starts

The year is 1935 and a single-decker bus seen here in the wet gloom of Manchester's Piccadilly is more a bone-shaker than cushioned comfort.

Gone are the days when a typical line-up of traffic at this corner of Portland Street would include a horse-drawn heavy lorry, a lighter horse-drawn cart, double-deck tram and single-deck bus. But Manchester's record for transport innovation has always been a proud one. The first bus route in Britain began in 1824 with a horse-bus service between

Manchester's Market Street and Pendleton and Salford. It cost sixpence for three miles. Manchester introduced horse-drawn trams in 1877 and the city's last tram ran in 1949 with the last trolley bus in 1966. Close to Piccadilly Gardens and not to be confused with the coach station at nearby Chorlton Street, the bus station has seen several attempts to transform it. Buses taking passengers across the city now leave from a Piccadilly that has had a major facelift which has affected architecture and garden design.

# Oxford Street's star attraction

The ultra-modern structure that stands where the Prince's Theatre used to be clearly has a long way to go before it can claim a place in Manchester's architectural archives.

Today, the spot in Oxford Street is dominated by multi-storey Peter House. But in the middle of the last century, it was the hub of theatreland and the Prince's was renowned for packing them in to see the stars of the day. The imposing and quietly-dignified theatre was opened on October 15, 1864 and at one time was managed by producer Robert Courtneidge. It was he, in 1902, who brought the great Sarah Bernhardt and her company from Paris for two special performances. It was star-studded shows such as these that helped Manchester gain a theatre tradition second only to London. The last performance at the Prince's was by the Arts Theatre Ballet on April 20, 1940 – the year the picture on the left was taken. It was to have been replaced by a new ABC cinema – but German bombs completed the demolition and wartime restrictions prevented any start on the new building. It is rumoured that Hitler himself had given orders not to bomb the nearby Midland Hotel. If so, precision bombing is nothing new, because the Germans managed to destroy the Free Trade Hall, just over 100 yards away and get a direct hit on the Prince's Theatre, which was across the road from the hotel. Truth is, this had more to do with bad luck than anything else, as the hits were actually achieved in darkness – and the Prince's Theatre was, perhaps, just a shade unlucky.

# 1940S-50S

## The Square that still oozes style

In the words of the classic crooners' standard, you either have or you haven't got style. As far back as 1709, the historic St Ann's Square had plenty when it was a select residential area of Manchester.

Today, the location is a byword for upmarket shopping. Although lying within the heart of a fashionable shopping district, the much-regarded Conservation Area rightly retains much of the character of the past – both in scale and landscape. The older image of St Ann's Square was taken in 1940, and in the years that have passed, the special

atmosphere and vitality has been enhanced by the removal of clutter and elimination of through traffic. Landscaping and pedestrianisation of the Square has made it a safer and more convenient method of shopping, returning to the more tranquil setting of medieval times. But even when surrounded by magnificent architecture, the stone bollards dotted around the square and designed to stop traffic entering, are equally as eye-catching. They raised eyebrows with their arrival in 1994 because critics felt they detracted from the elegant Georgian and Victorian buildings. However, a year later the "cannonball" bollards which dot the centre of the city like giant marbles, won a prestigious Street Design Award and judges voted St Ann's Square the best newly-pedestrianised area in the country.

# 1940S-50S

# Great deal is still on offer

A trip down Market Street has certainly changed over the last 60 years. In the Forties you could take the old heavy trams down one of Manchester's most famous shopping streets.

The old lines can clearly be seen in the image taken in 1940. The rails were last used as part of Manchester's original tramway system, which closed on January 10, 1949. Back then the original tramlines, which were laid between 1875 and 1880, ran down most of the old Victorian city centre streets. Ironically, they were removed to make way for the current

system in the 1990s. Nowadays the area is pedestrianised and while the mode of transport may have changed, shops are still as big an attraction as they were back then. Market Street was widened during 1821-22 for its present function as a principal shopping area. Where the popular J L Levy tailors once stood, a range of modern clothing stores represent the forefront of the Arndale Centre. The centre, which dominates the street, was completed in 1979 when it was the largest covered shopping centre in Europe. Architects Hugh Wilson and Lewis Womersley created the centre and they also redeveloped the University Precinct on Oxford Road and housing in Hulme. The dirty-yellow ceramic clad building has been criticised for its appearance over the years but is currently undergoing a major facelift. Owners Prudential are pumping £150m into the centre, including a £10m refurbishment of the southern part, including Market Street and the extensive redevelopment of the northern part.

# Victoria reigns but stays quiet

It is a famous view that has changed over the years – and the name of the road pictured is one that is rarely used now.

These photos – separated by 60 years – offer a view of Victoria Street, at the Manchester cathedral end of Deansgate, in the ever-evolving city centre. The photograph taken in 1946 – six years after the cathedral was bombed by the Luftwaffe and 50 years before the IRA detonated a bomb a few yards away from it – reveals how busy the area once was.

Buses, sleek cars and smartly-dressed men and women make their way down cobbled streets as the country recovers from the Second World War, with dark skies and chimneys in the background. The cathedral itself is covered with soot, but its intricate Gothic styling is unmistakable. Today's picture shows a quieter moment on a cleaner Victoria Street.

# 1940S-50S

## Tickets please!

The picture of Manchester's Omnibus bus station in 1948 should bring back happy memories for those who can recall why huge queues were regularly seen waiting patiently outside in the summer months.

For much of the 20th century, Mosley Street in the city centre meant buses, and in the holidays, it was the easiest and cheapest way for people to escape to the coast. Omnibus, one of the city's main bus stations, stood on the site now occupied by the Bridgewater Hall, from 1928 to 1973. Like a magnet, it drew holidaymakers in their droves, all excited that the next stop would be Blackpool

or north Wales. The bus station was flanked by an adult education centre and by Isherwoods Garages, where motorists could park for 10p a day. Sadly, the area between Lower Mosley Street and Great Bridgewater Street gradually became run down and neglected and when the bus station was demolished, the once-bustling setting became an ugly, sprawling car park. On a happier note, the future arrived in the shape of the G-MEX centre which saved nearby Central Station from oblivion. Similarly, the Bridgewater concert hall helped complete a transformation on a site that has witnessed many changes in 200 glorious years of history.

# A bridge to the past

In 1950, this stretch of the River Irwell was more an eyesore than an asset. Today, it proudly harbours a dazzling boom in city centre living and commerce.

In fact, these contrasting images appear to bridge a gap in time and style with impeccable ease. Sir Rocco Forte's five-star Lowry Hotel, opened in April 2001, is as much a showpiece landmark as the visionary Calatrava footbridge, which, importantly, links Salford to Manchester. When the steel bridge was being built in the late-90s – a deliberate

statement for the new Millennium – there were disused warehouses at the Salford end, and now the gleaming Lowry Hotel stands in their place. More than £100m of private and public investment went into regenerating the area, reportedly making it one of the region's most popular places to do business. Developments like the Inland Revenue building nearby have also helped dramatically reverse the decline, with plush new apartments mushrooming all around. The Lowry Hotel and the increase in residential projects reflect the attractiveness of the area to new investors and businesses.

# An art deco landmark that made the news

In nearly 50 years this view of Deansgate in Manchester city centre has changed dramatically.

The art deco Northcliffe House has been demolished as part of the £500m Spinningfields and Crown Square regeneration scheme, intended to breathe new life into the corner of Manchester, which spans from Deansgate to the River Irwell. In the 1956 image, pictured left, the art deco edifice can be seen towering in the background – a landmark structure built in

1932, which for years was the city base for the Daily Mail and Sunday People. By the autumn of 1970, the Manchester Evening News and the northern editions of the Guardian were also being produced from the site. But today, the Royal Bank of Scotland now occupies the site. The regeneration is very much work in progress, however, as the M.E.N.

building you see here will soon be no more. A new, state-of-the-art complex in the heart of the Spinningfields business district is currently being built, and will soon become the fourth home in the paper's history.

# 1940S-50S

# Furrowed brow

Perched next to the Mancunian Way is one of Manchester's symbols of 1960s modernisation.

But just a decade earlier Pin Mill Brow was part of a very different environment.

This picture of the gently rising brow in 1956 shows how much the area has changed. Back then, the skies were criss-crossed by wires used by the trolley buses that were rapidly replacing trams on many roads. Long gone are many of the chimneys and tall commercial buildings that

She's a
MACKESON type

...and all the better for it !

dominated the skyline and most buildings on the Limekiln Lane side of the brow, as well as many at the Ashton Old Road junction, have been demolished. Pin Mill Brow is now little more than a thoroughfare as trees and open spaces have taken over the urban sprawl. During the 19th century the area was famed for its historical significance. It is believed that a band which played at the infamous Peterloo Massacre fled to a pub near the brow for safety. The Lancashire yeomanry's killing of several of the 80,000 crowd that gathered at St Peter's Fields on August 16, 1819 to call for political reform has become a notorious incident in Britain's history.

# 1940s-50s

## Pub that fought on against last orders

It is almost 50 years ago that the picture below was taken, but many people still remember the Castle and Falcon pub in the Shudehill district of Manchester.

Before its demolition in 1996, real-ale buffs twice fought off attempts by transport chiefs to bulldoze the building that occupied the same spot in Bradshaw Street for 230 years. A top-floor blaze in 1990 seriously damaged the pub, one of the oldest in central Manchester, which was used as a lock-up for prisoners more than 200 years ago. The pub, which was

once a chapel with stained-glass windows, was finally levelled to make room for the Metrolink track, pictured right as we see it today. For many years, members of the Campaign for Real Ale fought to save the badly-neglected Castle and Falcon by promoting its use as a pub, but they lost out after engineers ruled that it was in too dangerous a state to

preserve. Today, the ultra-modern Metrolink dominates an area once heavily endowed with Victorian buildings, offices, warehouses and workshops. The area around Shudehill still has many other older buildings worth a passing glance.

# Changing face of the old guard

Old-style street lamps and rows of chimney stacks are a rare sight these days – but one structure in the heart of Manchester's Ardwick district has stood the test of time.

The former base of the Territorial Army's 252 Field Regiment, in Hyde Road, is soldiering on despite the changes that have taken place around it. The dark, brick building was used by the TA from 1947-1967.

The site next door carried an ad for Bovril. The same site today is occupied by another drinks ad – this time for Budweiser beer.

Nearby, is a vast building still under construction, believed to be a new cash-and-carry outlet or office complex.

# Picture palace rests in peace

Brothers Barry, Maurice and Robin Gibb would entertain a cinema full of rowdy kids with songs such as Lollipop, Book of Love and Putting On The Style.

But were they to go to the same venue years later, the brothers, better known as The Bee Gees, would be praying and not performing. It is the same building in Chorlton-cum-Hardy but there is now a funeral parlour where the old cinema used to be. And the purpose-built snooker hall has been replaced by a JD Wetherspoon pub. The image shows Manchester Road in

1958, when it was home to the popular suburban cinema the Gaumont. Originally opened as The Picture Palace in 1922, it changed its name to The Savoy in 1928 and was one of the first cinemas in suburban Manchester that could show the new talking pictures. The Gaumont also has the distinction of being the spot where the local Gibb Brothers first appeared on stage – years later they became the chart-topping Bee Gees. After the War, the Gaumont continued screening films but the bright and bustling cinema, which drew young and old, closed in about 1966 to begin a new lease of life as a funeral parlour, today run by the Co-op. The building, which used to be a focal point for the community's leisure activities, became sedate and sombre. Next door is the Sedge Lynn, which has been converted and restored to preserve some of the snooker hall's distinctive features.

# Standing test of time

South Manchester's Wheatsheaf Hotel has done well to survive the ravages of time.

Situated at the junction between Broom Lane and Stockport Road in Levenshulme, the imposing pub structure is as good an example as any of the changing face of the area through regeneration.

The mills and factories that were once a prominent feature of this south Manchester district have all but disappeared, and in their

place today is a lively and proud community feeding on the benefits of a multi-million-pound regeneration programme. It has brought renewed vigour to the vital Stockport Road corridor and reversed its decline. Old Levenshulme is remembered fondly by many for the number of its cinemas. The Arcadia and Palace were locally known as the "bug huts", and one was so close to the railway that when a train passed you couldn't hear the film. The Regal was a plush picture palace, and, just to show rowdy behaviour is no modern phenomena, the Kingsway was smashed up by the over-excited audience watching Rock Around The Clock. But times change and names come and go. The Arcadia became a cash-and-carry and the Grand cinema a furniture store.

# Changing fabric of society

The two photographs are separated by a good few years, but they are worlds apart and reflect just how Manchester has changed.

Barlow Moor Road in Chorlton-cum-Hardy is captured in post-war years, long before cars flooded the roads and became by far the most popular mode of transport. The photograph on the left shows a classic British car of the time as well as people waiting at a bus stop outside Leon's fabric shop. The shop – which continues to trade today from new

premises at 419 Barlow Moor Road – has been replaced by an apartment development called Chorlton Park. This distinctive creation was designed by Manchester architect Roger Stephenson and caused controversy among some local residents when it was first built. However, it reflected the new type of apartment that is now commonplace in the city and won Stephenson a clutch of awards including the prestige Stirling Prize for Housing Design. He was commissioned by the Irwell Valley Housing Association as part of a scheme to offer shared ownership to those struggling to get onto the property ladder. It was a challenge, because the site had also been a petrol station and the land was contaminated to a depth of three metres. His brief was to rethink the traditional way social housing was designed – and Chorlton Park has now become a landmark in the area.

# You must remember this...

The roundabout in Levenshulme, where Moseley Road, Kingsway and Birchfields Road meet - pictured in 1959.

The large building on the right of the older photograph was a cinema and is now gone, replaced by Apex House. But the Kingsway Hotel, half hidden by shrubbery in today's picture from the same angle, is still there.

# 1960s-70s

## Gateway to the future for vibrant city terminus

There are marked differences between these images of Manchester's Piccadilly Station Approach – and worth a close look at what they reveal about the architectural changes that have taken place.

Sadly, not all the alterations to the landscape we can see today were welcomed at first, including the decision to build the luxury Malmaison Hotel, pictured right, on the site once occupied by both the historic Joshua Hoyle Building, and the Imperial Hotel, a Grade II listed pub. The older photograph taken in 1960 clearly shows that at

the time a large stretch of London Road really was in need of a facelift. Needless to say, critics of the improvements were not slow in slamming the destruction of the seven-

storey Edwardian warehouse. Today, the famous gateway to the city highlights how the area has been transformed from ageing hub to vibrant city centre railway terminus.

# Soccer fans are court on camera

Football fans wearing flat caps and knee-length overcoats form an orderly queue for buses to the opening matches of the 1960 season... while the modern-day picture could not be more different.

While the old buses were packed full and the journey to the grounds was often uncomfortable, today's fans travel in relative luxury. Times have changed for fans and the historic building in the background has also been transformed. The ornate Solway House in Aytoun Street, built in 1875 as a police station and court, has had a £15 million

refurbishment to become the Minshull Street court complex. For more than 100 years, the building with its landmark clock tower and snarling beast statues had its fair share of famous cases. Among those who appeared in the dock was Walter Graham Rowland, who was later hanged at Strangeways in 1947 for murder. Before his execution, another prisoner hanged himself in his cell after confessing that he had committed the murder and not Rowland. Today, trams travel the street and the building houses 10 courtrooms and accommodation for barristers, judges and jurors.

# 1960s-70s

# Grimy road gets a clean-up

Hard to believe that the photograph below was taken as recently as 1962.

Then, Henrietta Street, just off Stretford Road in Old Trafford, was a typically grimy example of a sooty, northern city.

However, the row of buildings in the centre of the picture are still standing, seemingly in better condition than they were back then.

Not a lot has changed on Stretford Road itself; trees have sprung up at the road

junction and the street
furniture is slightly different...
as are the cars. Note that not
many women do their
shopping in headscarves
these days!

HENRIETTA
STREET

# Jewel in the Crown

Time has changed the appearance of this corner of Booth Street – but the Crown Hotel name continues to reign in the heart of Manchester city centre.

The older image of the hotel, taken in 1962, will probably bring memories flooding back for anyone who worked in the city's rapidly-growing corporate and banking district off Spring Gardens. It may look very different, but a walk around the immediate area is a must for those with an appreciation of the city's architectural mix and heritage. The modern

columns below a towering office block, pictured in the updated image, and the buildings visible in the background are more in keeping with the style of this commercial quarter of the city. Looking like a mini-Manhattan, closer inspection of some of the buildings reveals everything from rusticated stone and red brick, to arcade openings and marble-lined walls. In fact, the real crowning glory of many of the buildings can't actually be appreciated from the outside.

A look inside one of the banks, since converted to a pub, reveals that some of the original furnishings have been retained, such as customer writing cubicles and polished granite columns. Nearby, other imposing bank and insurance buildings all happily conspire to help signal the city's financial prowess and convey the successful commercial magnet it is today.

# 1960s-70s

## Same place, different world

Here is one of Manchester's most famous streets before it achieved its iconic status. Left, is Canal Street in 1963, then a nondescript back street alongside the Rochdale Canal.

Right, is Canal Street today, one of the most vibrant entertainment areas in Manchester – albeit at night – and the heart of the city's Gay Village. Not much has physically changed in the 40-odd years between the two pictures. Industry and businesses have moved out of the buildings and bars, clubs and restaurants have moved in, but the street scene

remains largely the same. However, note that the Tarmac in 1963 has now been ripped up to expose the cobbles which the city father of the 1960s obviously thought were rather old-fashioned.

# 1960s-70s

# Stuck in the past

With no fewer than seven cars visible idly blocking the pavement, it seems finding a free parking space round Manchester was as much a problem in 1963 as it is today.

A Hillman Minx, Triumph Herald and Morris Traveller – all very popular cars in their day – are among the stationary vehicles pictured here in the older image. It all demonstrates just how much the car had become an intimate part of life for everyone in the so-called Swinging Sixties. A poster hanging outside the Birch Park Skating Palace advertises

a forthcoming concert by Brian Poole and the Tremeloes. This is a real memory jerker for fans of the London pop outfit around at the time of the emerging Beatles and Rolling Stones. Today, the busy location – at Anson Road, close to the Dickenson Road junction, in Fallowfield – shows little sign of change to the surroundings and

architecture, despite a gap of more than 40 years between the two pictures. Where the renowned roller rink and Hanson greengrocers once stood is now the hub of shopping for people living at nearby Longsight, Rusholme and Birchfields Park. The parade of shops includes Venus Foods, an exotic food centre that not only benefits from its position at the heart

of a vibrant residential area, but also attracts plenty of customers from its spot just two miles south of Manchester city centre.

# Pubs' links with the Italians' jobs

At first sight, these pictures seem to have little connection with Manchester's historic links with Italy.

But on closer inspection, the name of the pub, The Milan Inn, gives a clue to the role Italian immigrants played in the city.

The pub, at the junction of Rochdale Road and Queens Road in Harpurhey, was pictured in 1966. It was the site of the home of the Peduzzi family, who arrived in the city around the turn of the 19th century from a small

village in the State of Lombardy, where Milan was capital. They were one of a group of pioneer immigrant families from northern Italy, who were very skilled craftsmen and brought their expertise with them to Manchester. They soon started in business as woodcarvers and makers of picture frames, looking glasses, barometers and scientific instruments. But they were not the only Italians to arrive in the city as the cotton trade lured hundreds to settle in Ancoats. So many made the area their home it became dubbed Little Italy, and Ancoats became one of the most cosmopolitan areas of Manchester. Today new homes have been built next to the Milan Inn, but the pub remains the same and its name bears testimony to the area's links with Italy.

# 1960s-70s

# A new approach

These two contrasting images show an area of Manchester frequently seen by commuters and visitors to the city.

When visitors to Manchester first got off the train at Piccadilly Station this was one of the first buildings they would see – the imposing London Road Station Warehouse on the corner of Ducie Street in 1966.

Now, of course, Piccadilly Approach has been spruced up and the warehouse in the background has been turned

into a smart apartment hotel
with the Cotton House
restaurant on the ground floor.

# Changing guard at the Palace

The years may have rolled on but Levenshulme Palace still offers a right royal night out.

Originally called The Palace Cinema, it has been the Palace Nightclub for the past decade, and remains very much at the heart of the local community where it is a key venue for live bands, comedy, sport and all things Irish. In its early days when the "flicks" reigned supreme, it was one of no fewer than five cinemas in the area. Known affectionately as either the

Farmside, because of its location in Farmside Close, or the Bug Hut, it was a regular haunt every week for hundreds of cinema lovers. In the '20s, Rudolph Valentino was the romantic star of the age, in the '50s Teddy Boys in their drainpipe trousers and string ties held sway – often gathering at nearby Sivori's ice cream parlour before shows. Both The Palace and another local cinema, The Arcadia, were built alongside the main railway embankment and long before Bill Haley and his Comets had picture houses shaking, passing trains made both venues shake, rattle and roll. The archive photograph taken in 1971 shows the cinema and the old town market. The market has long since disappeared, and although The Palace closed to filmgoers in 1984, the venue still enjoys a role at the centre of the community.

# 1960s-70s

# The magic of St Mary's

When all around was changing, St Mary's Church in Hulme survived to witness what was arguably the most ambitious exercise in community architecture ever seen in Britain.

In fact, from the tallest church spire in Manchester, it would have been easy to survey showpiece new housing replacing the much-derided deck-access flats that once dominated the district. Today, the quality of urban design is more lively, a mixture of living space, shops and cafes – in contrast to the demolished high-density homes of the 1970s. A walk

further along Chichester Road, seen in the pictures, would take you past imaginative, individual structures, with courtyards, curved roofs and the use of cream brick to add to the overall brightness of an increasingly-popular suburb. The mid-Victorian listed church is not the only building that remained to become part of a bright new future for the Hulme area. Nearby is Loreto sixth form college – formerly Loreto Convent, started by an order of nuns in 1851 – which caters for young people of different faiths.

# 1960s-70s

## How the Lake was left high and dry

In its day, Belle Vue was one of the premier tourist attractions in the north west – but who would have believed that this residential area of east Manchester once boasted a picturesque boating lake?

The landmark Lake Hotel, on Hyde Road, Gorton, was named after it, and was opened in 1876 to take advantage of the nearby Belle Vue railway station. A popular venue through the years for the thousands of visitors to the giant Belle Vue zoo and park complex, the hotel remained open long after the latter was closed in 1977. The archive picture shows the

Lake Hotel in 1971. The building was eventually demolished to make way for new housing, with its architectural secrets thoughtfully mounted on oilskin at Manchester's Chetham's Library. Today, most of the old amusement park location near to where the hotel once stood has been replaced by housing, plus a £6m multi-screen cinema.

free internet access . family history . talking books . business information . talks . art . homework centres . language courses . theatre . help for inventors . DVDs . free events for kids . festivals . silver surfer clubs . local images collection . bestsellers . author visits . CDs . free computing courses . newspapers . mobiles . community information . brilliant books . displays . on-line learning . reading groups . CD-ROMs . culture . local history . books for babies . exhibitions . advice . workshops . live poetry . sheet music . what's on . treasures . coffee . videos . storytimes . fun

# When did you last visit *your* library?

## www.manchester.gov.uk/libraries

manchester library
& information service

MANCHESTER
CITY COUNCIL